Richard Z

Richard Zajdlic combines a car
writer. His previous plays inclu
and *Cannibal* (both with Rich:
which won the West London Playw.....
1991, and *Rage*. He has also written for *Eastenders*,
London's Burning and *This Life*.

RICHARD ZAJDLIC

Dogs Barking

faber and faber

First published in 1999
by Faber and Faber Limited
3 Queen Square, London WC1N 3AU

Typeset by Country Setting, Kingsdown, Kent CT14 8ES
Printed and bound by CPI Antony Rowe, Eastbourne

A CIP record for this book
is available from the British Library

ISBN 978-0571-200061

2 4 6 8 10 9 7 5 3 1

Dogs Barking was first performed at the Bush Theatre, London, on 5 May 1999, with the following cast:

Vicky Caroline Catz
Alex Raquel Cassidy
Neil Tony Curran
Splodge Tony Maudsley

Director Mike Bradwell
Designer Natalie Gibbs
Lighting Designer Aideen Malone
Assistant Director Nicola Parry

Characters

Alex
Neil
Ray
Vicky

Act One (Saturday)

Morning. The kitchen/living room area of an open-plan one-bedroom flat. Neil, early thirties, is asleep on the pull-down sofa bed, a sheet and blanket half-tossed over his body. His clothes lie scattered on the floor amidst a few strewn magazines and papers. A nearly full wine bottle sits on the floor next to a coffee table littered with spliff remnants, ashtray, fag packet, lighter, rizlas etc . . . The curtains are closed though a gleam of daylight can be seen through the gap. The door to the bedroom opens and Alex enters. She is in her early thirties, wearing a silk dressing gown. She pulls a brush through her hair as she looks at the comatose figure on the sofa. She scans the room with distaste before moving to the window to open the curtains. Neil reacts vampire-like to the daylight. Alex moves into the kitchen area and turns the radio on. She switches the kettle on then pours herself a bowl of muesli. Neil groans and sits up gingerly, reaching for his cigarettes. He lights one up and smokes silently for a while, brooding. Alex remains in the kitchen area, munching her cereal, watching him. Neil has his back to her but can sense her scrutiny.

Alex Do you want some breakfast?

Neil Having it. Thanks.

  Silence. Alex eats. Neil smokes.

Alex How's your head?

Neil Busy.

Alex I'm meeting someone in town at eleven.

Neil Yeah?

Alex You'll have to leave when I do. Okay? Neil?

Neil What?

Alex You've got about quarter of an hour.

Neil I can't clear this up in fifteen minutes.

Alex I'm not asking you to. I'm asking you to get dressed. And leave. I'll do it later.

Neil laughs at that. Silence. Alex eats. Neil smokes.

Did you sleep okay?

Neil You mean, under the circumstances?

Alex I didn't invite you here –

Neil I slept fine. Thanks. You?

Alex Fine.

Neil Good.

Alex looks at her muesli – it's a real effort. She takes a final mouthful, then dumps the bowl in the sink. She makes herself a cup of instant coffee.

Alex There's coffee if you want some.

Neil Great.

Alex Decaffinated.

Neil Great.

Alex Help yourself.

Neil picks up his cigarette packet and counts how many he has left: not enough. Alex turns the radio off, takes her coffee and heads towards the bedroom.

Neil Can you get me some fags while you're gone?

Alex stops, giving him a look which he chooses to misinterpret.

Neil I'll pay you back.

Alex What do you want, Neil?

Neil Marlboro's fine. Or Camels. None of that 'Lights' shit though –

Alex What are you doing here? What do you want? Really?

Neil takes a final drag and stubs his cigarette out.

Neil The toilet.

Alex What?

Neil I'm busting. D'you mind?

Alex moves away from the door, irritated.

Alex Hurry up, then.

Neil I'd go in the sink but it's number twos, you know?

Alex That's very considerate, thank you.

Neil Isn't it? I had to use this last night.

He holds up the nearly full bottle of wine, equally exasperated.

Do you always lock the bedroom door?

Alex Not always.

Neil And you didn't hear me knocking? I just wanted a piss, Alex. I wasn't trying to come in for any other reason. You think that's why I'm here? For that? (*Laughs.*) It's gone beyond that, don't you think?

Alex I don't know.

Neil You wouldn't have let me in here if it hadn't.

Alex I've done it before.

Neil Not this time.

Alex No.

A stand-off.

I thought you needed the toilet?

Neil If that's what you want.

He picks up the wine bottle and stands up. He's naked. He gestures to his flaccid penis.

Not too insulting, I hope.

Neil goes into the bedroom. Alex puts her coffee down and moves to the sofa-bed to strip the bedding. She takes the blanket and starts to fold it then hurls it furiously down. A moment while she calms herself, then begins again, folding the bedding up in an anally neat fashion. The toilet flushes. She hoists the bed back into it's sofa state, then picks up the magazines and newspapers, expecting Neil to appear. He doesn't. She moves to the bedroom door.

Alex Neil?

Neil *(off)* I'm in the bedroom. Is this what you're going to wear?

Alex What?

Neil enters, wearing a towel round his torso and carrying a black dress.

Neil For your date. This black number. It's new, isn't it?

Alex goes to take it but he moves away from her.

Alex Don't crease it –

Neil Bit over the top for a Saturday morning –

Alex I'm taking it back to the shop.

Neil Yeah, I didn't think you were a size ten.

Alex Can I have it, please?

Neil How come you didn't try it on beforehand? Present, right?

He explores it admiringly.

Not bad. You're sucking a better class of dick now, obviously.

Alex Who said it was from a man?

Neil That's her aftershave in the bathroom, is it? Expensive stuff.

Alex May I?

He passes the dress over. She takes it, picks up the blanket and sheet, and goes back into the bedroom, closing the door.

Neil You didn't lock it. Aren't you worried I might come in?

The bedroom door is locked. Neil reaches behind his back and pulls out from under his towel Alex's purse which he's tucked there during his trip to the bathroom. He moves to the sofa, taking the purse and her coffee with him. He sits, lights another cigarette and starts to examine the contents of the purse as he talks, finding a condom, money, credit cards, some receipts and business cards – all of which he studies carefully before replacing.

So, who is it then? Alex?

Alex (*off*) What?

Neil I said, who is it? That you're meeting. Are you embarrassed? Is that it? What is he? Nice and decent but not quite the 'fuck-you' alternative you hoped for?

Silence. Neil takes a sip of coffee, grimacing in disgust.

You want to take a good look at what's happening here. You know? There is a definite trend towards the anaemic. Caffeine-free fucking coffee? What's that about?

Alex (*off*) Personal choice.

Neil Fine for you – what about normal people?

Alex (*off*) Do you know any?

Neil And where's all the drugs? There is nothing chemical in that bathroom at all. Nothing. Tiger balm bollocks – where's all the synthetics? Aspirin? Paracetamol? Just because you're immune to life's biological little warfares doesn't mean your guests won't need some attention.

Alex (*off*) You're not a guest.

He pulls out a small passport-style photo. He studies it carefully.

Neil Is it someone I know? Is that why you won't say?

He broods for a beat then puts the photo back and lays the purse on the table. He goes to take another sip of coffee, decides against it and gets up, irritated.

There must be something here. That stuff for your periods. Feminax.

Alex (*off*) I don't use it anymore.

He moves to the kitchen area and throws the offending drink down the sink. He starts to look noisily through her cupboards as Alex comes out of the bedroom, fully clothed, carrying a shoulder-bag and the black dress.

Are you dressed yet?

Neil Um . . .

Alex Two minutes.

She lays the dress down on the back of the sofa and starts to check through her shoulder-bag for her purse. She looks up, unable to find it. She scans the room and sees it lying on the table. She gives Neil a look as she picks it up.

Find anything?

Neil Not much. Lot of restaurant receipts. Better than we ever went to.

Alex Hurts, doesn't it?

She starts to check through the contents of her purse.

Neil You must be doing well.

Alex I get by.

Neil New job?

Alex I'd start getting ready if I were you.

Neil Expense account, definitely.

Alex One minute.

She drops the purse in her bag and moves to the door to get her coat.

Neil I need a shower first.

Alex Too late.

Neil I stink.

Alex puts her coat on and starts to gather up Neil's clothes. Neil stubs his cigarette out in the sink and crosses towards her.

Look. Why don't you go? I'll tidy up, have a wash, let myself out.

Alex You can put them on in here or in the street. It's your choice.

Neil I thought we were going to talk?

Alex Last night we were going to talk.

Neil I was pissed.

Alex Apparently, yes.

Neil I thought we'd have now. This morning.

Alex I'm meeting someone.

Neil Who?

Alex It's none of your business.

Neil Well, obviously, that's why I'm interested. (*Beat.*) I could always follow you. Find out that way.

Alex dumps the clothes at his feet.

Alex Fine. Follow me. Just get dressed and –

Neil (*laughs*) Oh, for fuck's sake, Alex. Make it up. Just make it up, okay? Humour me. Say, it's John. I'm meeting John. Or Andrew. Ben. Michael, anyone – I won't know, will I?

Alex Is that what you're worried about? That's it's Ben?

Neil Depends when it started.

Alex When would you have liked it to start?

Neil So it is him?

Alex I'm not doing this –

Alex moves to get her bag and dress. Neil grabs her, pulling her round to face him.

Neil Are you fucking him or not?

Alex waits for him to let her go. He does. She collects her dress, folds it carefully and puts it in her bag. She picks the bag up and turns to face him.

Alex Here's what's going to happen. I'm going to go. Do whatever it is I've got to do and then come back. If you're still here by then, I'll call the police.

Neil They don't get involved in domestics.

Alex This isn't a domestic. It's trespassing.

Neil That's not what the lease says.

Alex is knocked back by that. Neil stoops and picks up the bundle of clothes.

Alex What did you say?

Neil It's half past ten. You'd better get going.

Alex This is my place.

Neil You'll be late.

Alex Mine.

Neil He'll think you've stood him up.

Alex We agreed this months ago.

Neil Don't get hysterical.

Alex I'm not. You said. You told me –

Neil I don't remember saying a fucking thing. You talked. You decided. That's what I remember. This great assumption that, somehow, retaining some integrity

would mean more to me than keeping my options open.
It doesn't. Sorry. Nice try, though. Thanks.

They stare at each other, both a little choked.

Alex So that's it, is it? The money?

*Neil heads off towards the bedroom, taking his
clothes with him.*

Neil I'm going to have a shower. Get some kip. I didn't
sleep much last night.

Alex drops her bag and pursues him to the doorway.

Alex You're not having this flat.

Neil Just half.

Alex You're not entitled. I paid for it. I'm the one who
kept it going.

Neil Don't forget the fags.

He closes the door, locking it.

Alex Neil?

She tries the door then bangs on it, furious.

You promised me. You promised!

Neil (*off*) I'll be out in a few hours. We'll talk then.

Alex Now. You're not doing this. I'm not letting you do
this. D'you hear me? Neil?

*The sound of the shower starts up along with Neil
singing. Alex cries out in utter frustration, thumping
the door, fighting the urge to smash it down and
batter him senseless. She takes a moment to compose
herself, checks her watch, curses: she's running very
late. She debates what to do next, torn. A decision.
She picks up her bag and starts to go, stops, returning*

to take Neil's cigarette packet and lighter from the coffee table: a small revenge. She puts them in her pocket and goes, slamming the front door behind her. Fade to black.

SCENE TWO

Afternoon. The light outside is dull, overcast. Neil is sitting on the sofa, talking on the phone. A 'Yellow Pages' directory lies open on the coffee table. A trunk sits near the bookcase into which various items have already been packed. Several books lay scattered on the floor.

Neil Yes, we bought it from you originally. About three years ago. Neil Ryder. With a 'y'. And my partner's name is Whelan. Alex. Female. It's a joint mortgage, yes. That's right.

The intercom buzzer sounds. Neil looks round but otherwise ignores it.

No, this afternoon's a bit tricky. Next week? Morning preferably. Yes, I work from home so that's no problem –

The intercom buzzer is sounding again. Repeatedly. Neil shows his irritation.

Excuse me. One second.

He gets up and crosses to the door. He presses the intercom switch to speak.

Hello?

Ray (*off*) It's me. Splodge.

Neil Took your time, didn't you?

Neil presses the buzzer to open the downstairs door. He holds it for a beat, leaves the door to the flat ajar

17

*and returns to the phone as the intercom buzzer
sounds again. Neil returns to the intercom, presses the
switch to speak.*

Neil Push the door. When the buzzer sounds –

Ray (*off*) Yeah, give us a fucking chance then.

*Neil presses the buzzer again, holds it for a long beat
then returns to the phone.*

Neil Sorry about that. Monday, yes? Eleven o'clock.
That's great. Yes. 0181-445-8774. See you then. Bye.

*Neil puts the phone down, pausing a moment to
reflect on the action taken. He shuts the 'Yellow
Pages' book, replaces it on the shelf under the coffee
table then gets up and moves back to the trunk to
resume packing books. Ray enters: early thirties, large
frame, running rapidly to fat. He's carrying a plastic
bag full of beer cans and crisps/chocolate.*

Ray Don't mention the lift's fucked, will you?

Neil It's only two flights.

Ray And the rest, you cunt. Two levels, maybe, but it's
four flights at least. And I'm carrying stuff.

*Ray shuts the door and moves to the kitchen to dump
the bag on one of the unit tops.*

Neil This is a first, Splodge. You coming in and
whingeing about something. I barely recognise you.

Ray Yeah, alright. I've got grounds though, ain't I?

*Ray helps himself to a lager as Neil comes across to
sift through the contents of the bag.*

Bastard doctor's taken me off the steroids.

Neil How come?

Ray Cos he's a fucking Nazi, that's why. Says he'll only give me another injection if I lose a stone in weight. That's illegal, innit? He can't do that.

Neil Where are the fags?

Ray fishes out a packet from his coat pocket and hands them over as he talks.

Ray You can't go fucking with a man's pain threshold – what sort of a psycho, does that?

Neil Matches?

Neil tosses the packet down onto the unit top as Ray does the honours with a lighter.

Ray Says he's trying to motivate me into adopting a more healthy, self-help kind of attitude.

Neil Ta.

Neil moves back to finish packing the books. Ray helps himself to a cigarette as he talks.

Ray It's just sick, innit? That ain't helping me. All that's motivating is the urge to kick his fucking head in. I mean, what's the point? Dieting ain't going to change nothing.

Neil No?

Ray No, 'course it ain't.

Neil You don't think being a fat bastard's a contributing factor?

Ray That's bone on bone, that is. (*knee joint*) There's no cartilage in there. I walk on that it's going to hurt, innit? It don't matter how heavy I am, it's still going to fucking hurt. I'll still need the fucking painkillers, won't I?

Neil has finished packing the books. He checks his watch and heads off to the bedroom.

Neil You're right, Splodge. He's an ignorant man.

Ray Ignorant dead man, more like.

Ray heads for the sofa with his beer and cigarette.

And I ain't a fat bastard, neither.

Neil returns with two suitcases which he carries over to the front door.

What are you doing?

Neil Just shifting some stuff. You don't mind, do you?

Ray Eh?

Neil Taking them with you. It's just these and the trunk. I thought we could stash them at your Mum's place. In the garage. That's not a problem, is it?

Neil puts the cases down and goes to the kitchen to get out a number of plastic carrier bags.

Ray Well, I don't know.

Neil It's only temporary – 'til we get ourselves a bit settled.

Ray What's in them?

Neil Clothes mainly. Bits and pieces. Thought we'd best have a clear-out. Get rid of all the crap. Won't be room for any of my stuff otherwise.

Ray I can't help with the carrying –

Neil Yes, I've realised that. 'S okay. I need you up here anyway. Buzz me back in.

Ray Ain't you got a key?

Neil Not yet, no. Alex changed the locks, didn't she?

Ray nods, confused. He watches as Neil takes a plastic bag and starts to clear the shelf unit of Alex's collection of china animals and assorted bric-a-brac.

Ray She out then, is she? Alex.

Neil That's right.

Ray Bit of a turn-up, innit? Taking you back.

Neil More inevitable really.

Ray I thought you were with that Caroline bird?

Neil Not for a while now. Got a bit clingy, you know?

Ray You mean, she dumped you? (*Laughs.*) You should have brought her down the club. Introduce her to some real men.

Neil laughs, despite himself.

We never did get to meet her though, did we?

Neil Other way round, I think.

Ray She can't have been that ugly. You wouldn't have passed up Alex for some sweaty old Doris, would you?

Neil dumps the loaded bag into the trunk, opening another to continue.

Neil What about you? You getting it out much? Aside from to piss with, I mean.

Ray Oh, you know. Have me moments. I've got a house-wife in Brentford looks possible.

Neil Still fitting, yes?

Ray Fucking nightmare it is. She's having a kitchen in the Wolsey traditional, burgundy red. It's gonna suck all the light in, make the place look even pokier than it is. Should've had it in pastels at least, try and lift it up out of itself . . . what?

Neil (*grinning*) Nothing.

Ray 'S not funny. If she ain't satisfied she'll complain to the company. I ain't staff anymore. 'S all short-term contracts now, innit? Fuck up once and you're out.

Neil Well, make sure she is satisfied.

He holds his hand out, palm up and waggles his middle finger in a sexual gesture.

Ray (*laughs*) Yeah. I could, couldn't I? (*Beat.*) Not getting the signs though, you know? I think she's just being friendly.

Neil dumps the second bag into the trunk and crosses to the stereo unit to start packing Alex's record and CD collection into another bag.

Neil What sort of friendly?

Ray Cups of tea. Bit of cake. Just chatting really.

He watches Neil pack, increasingly troubled.

You chucking them out as well?

Neil Everything. Have a look through them if you like. See if there's anything you fancy.

Ray (*uncertain*) Yeah, I will. Ta.

Neil Same with the clothes. You find a bra your size, you take it – no questions asked.

Ray (*laughs*) Yeah, you'd like me in that, wouldn't you? You fucking perv.

Neil You'll try one on, don't pretend otherwise.

Ray Nah. I go for the panties, me. Nothing like a bit of snatch cloth to get you going, eh? (*Sniffs. Laughs.*) No offence.

Neil starts filling a second bag. Ray broods on the curiousness of it all.

So, when'd all this happen then? With Alex.

Neil Last night.

Ray Yeah? What? You just turned up and . . .

Neil Pretty much.

Ray No, go on, what? What d'you say to her?

Neil I don't know. We just talked. Bottle of wine. Went to bed.

Ray thinks about that. Neil continues packing.

Ray D'you fuck her?

Neil What?

Ray Did you?

Neil laughs and takes the two bags of CDs/cassettes over to the trunk.

What? What's wrong with that? I want to know. Did you have sexual intercourse? You did, didn't you? I bet you were fucking like dogs all night. Eh?

Ray does a very vocal re-enactment of the supposed frenzied action. Neil is scanning the room for other things to pack. He stops, studying Ray not unsympathetically.

Neil It's been quite a while for you, hasn't it Splodge?

Ray I can't tell you. I'd have you if you bent over long enough.

Neil laughs and moves to start taking down the pictures on the walls: glass-framed and blu-tacked posters alike. Ray watches, very troubled. He stands and goes to get himself some chocolate. Neil strips the walls.

Look, I ain't being funny, right?

Neil Okay.

Ray But, she does know about this, don't she? I mean, Alex. She does know what you're doing here.

Neil Yes, of course. Why?

Ray 'S a bit wholesale, innit?

Neil We're making a fresh start. New beginning, see? It was her idea. Get everything out. Build it up again from scratch. Left me to do it all, of course, while she goes shopping. (*Laughs.*) So not that fucking new, eh?

Silence. Neil removes pictures. Ray drinks lager, eats chocolate.

Ray I heard she was seeing someone.

Neil Ben Morris?

Ray I don't know –

Neil That's who I heard it was. Who did you hear?

Ray No-one particular. Just that she was –

Neil It's Ben Morris.

Ray Oh right. Who is he?

Neil Friend of mine. You don't know him.

Neil takes the pictures back to the trunk. Ray considers the new information.

Ray Well, okay. Him then. What's happening with that?

Neil Not my problem, is it?

Neil packs the pictures, a little roughly. He stops, brooding angrily.

She was screwing him before we split up. D'you know that? (*Scoffs.*) Sounds familiar, doesn't it?

He continues packing, then starts to close the trunk, fasten the clasps.

Neil Where are you parked? Round the back?

Ray Side. Liskin Street.

Neil Give us the keys then.

Ray thinks about that as Neil checks his watch again and gets up.

Splodge? Keys?

He approaches, hand outstretched in expectation. Ray gets the keys out but keeps hold of them, fingering them awkwardly.

Ray Look. What's going on, eh? I mean, I ain't seen you for weeks, then you tell me to come round. Say you're back with Alex.

Neil That's right.

Ray You're taking all her stuff.

Neil Storing it, yes.

Ray It's a bit odd though, innit? I wouldn't get rid of my albums.

Neil If it's what she wants –

Ray And them china things. She loves all them.

Neil You know what she loves now, do you?

Ray I ain't saying that –

Neil Then what?

Ray Well, ain't you gonna wait for her to come back? Check it over.

Neil What for?

Ray See if there's anything she wants to keep.

Neil She's already told me what to get rid of. (*Beat.*) What?

Ray I don't get it, that's all. I mean, what's the rush?

Neil I promised her I'd have it done.

Ray You have though, ain't you? It's all packed up. Ready.

Neil It's not in the van, is it?

Ray Take us five minutes to do that. (*Beat.*) Look, why don't we watch the match, eh? Wait for her to come back – I ain't seen her in ages – be nice, that. Say hello. What d'you reckon, eh? (*Beat.*) Come on. Let's stick the box on. Have a few beers. 'S why I brought the cans, innit? Yeah?

> *Ray sits and uses the remote to switch the TV on: a rugby match is being broadcast. Neil walks off to the kitchen to get himself a lager. He takes a few swigs, deliberating. Ray keeps a wary half-eye on him. Neil comes back and switches off the TV.*

Neil Okay. You want to know what's going on? I'm doing exactly what you should have done. With Gail.

Ray Eh?

Neil Don't leave the house. Remember? If you leave the house, you'll lose it all. Everything. I told you that. She was the one fucking around.

Ray Yeah, alright –

Neil She was the one who should've walked. Not you.

Ray It weren't as easy as that –

Neil It was for her, obviously.

Ray I had the kids to think about –

Neil Not any more, you don't. They've got a new Dad now.

Ray I'm their Dad.

Neil Not day to day. Not like the other bloke.

Ray I'm still their Dad.

Neil She kept the house, the kids, your wage packet – what did you keep? Your pride, of course. Self-respect.

Ray Fuck you.

Neil You should've smashed her face in. Battered her so hard that when she looked in a mirror she couldn't recognise herself. Maybe then she'd have understood how you felt, eh? Looking at her. Not knowing who the fuck she was any more. (*Beat.*) You had a deal, Splodge. If she didn't want to screw you any more then fine, but she should've lost something she did want. Something screwing you gave her. You can't have it all. Someone should teach her that.

> *Ray shifts uncomfortably, waiting until he can look Neil in the eye.*

Ray And that's what you're doing, is it? With Alex?

Neil If you like.

Ray What? By nicking her stuff?

Neil She'll get it back. It's a bit of pressure, that's all.

Help keep her focused on the fact that what I want is just as important as her fucking wish-list. Well?

Ray agonises a bit, squirming with indecision.

Ray What d'you get me involved for?

Neil Because I thought you'd understand. And I needed your van.

Ray Well, fucking hire one then.

Neil I'm banned, aren't I? Still six months off.

Ray I don't believe this.

Ray stresses out, going on an agitated walkabout.

Why didn't you ask Mickey? He's got a van.

Neil He wouldn't have come.

Ray Well, nor would I if I'd known what it was about.

Ray paces some more, stressing. Neil crosses to hold Ray still.

Neil Splodge, listen to me. Time is a factor here. Okay? We need to get this stuff out before Alex comes back with her boyfriend. Ben.

Ray Why? What's he like?

Neil Vindictive. He'll have about six of his mates with him – all ready to kick the living crap out of us.

Ray What d'you mean, 'us'? I ain't got nothing to do with it.

Neil Well, I'll try to explain that, of course.

Ray I can't get involved in violence. I've got a bad knee.

Ray starts heading for the door.

No, no, I'm sorry, mate. I mean, I'd like to help out but . . .

Neil stops him, gently but firmly.

Neil Take us five minutes. You said that yourself.

Ray I can't –

Neil We'll load up. You can drive off. And that's it. No-one's going to get famous. Alex won't even know you've been here.

Ray What if she finds out?

Neil She won't.

Ray Yeah, but what if –

Neil For fuck's sake, Splodge. Try to understand. The clock is ticking. If we don't shift this stuff, right now, we're going to still be here when Mr Meathead and the boys come charging in to stomp our fucking balls off. I think that means we should shift the stuff – what do you think?

Ray I think I should walk out. Leave you to it.

Neil I know that. But you're my friend. And I love you.

They laugh. Ray's resistance crumbles and he hands Neil the keys.

Good man.

Ray Just hurry it up, alright?

Ray opens the door as Neil picks up the two suitcases.

Neil It's the button by the intercom.

Ray Eh?

Neil For the door. Buzzing me back –

Ray Yeah, yeah, I know – go on, get on with it, will you?

Neil grins and goes. Ray stresses on the situation. He drinks lager, curses, lights another cigarette whether he needs to or not. Neil comes back into the room, still with the suitcases.

Neil Fuck it.

Ray What? (*Realises.*) You're joking.

Neil Heard her voice on the stairwell.

Neil has closed the door and is taking the suitcases back into the bedroom. Ray panics.

Ray Well, what are we going to do? What the fuck are we going to do now? Oh, Jesus – how many of them were there?

Neil (*off*) I couldn't tell.

Ray I bet there's hundreds. Well, that's it, innit? We're going to die. We are going to fucking die.

Neil returns and heads for the trunk.

Neil Get a grip, Splodge. Why don't you start telling me how tough you are? You're usually pretty fucking eloquent on the subject.

Ray I've got a bad knee though, ain't I?

Neil takes hold of the trunk to move. Ray rushes to help.

Yeah, good plan. What are we doing? Barricading the door?

Neil Just take your beer and sit down. Put the tele on. And don't do or say anything until I do.

Neil shoves the trunk to one side, against the wall. Ray switches the TV on with the remote and moves to the kitchen to find a weapon of some sort. He picks up a beer can.

Ray I should've brought bottles. We could've threatened to glass them. Make 'em back off 'til we –

Neil crosses to the unit to light himself a cigarette.

Neil Splodge. Relax. It's all perfectly innocent. You've just come round here for a chat, watch the game.

Ray That's all I fucking did come round here for an' all.

Neil quietens him as they hear indistinct voices outside. Ray continues to search for a cudgel of some sort. Neil goes and sits on the sofa to watch the game. The door opens and Alex enters, followed by Vicky: late twenties, well-groomed, attractive, with a better figure than her sister. She is carrying an overnight bag plus a few shopping bags bearing the logos of good quality clothing stores. A moment while everyone takes stock of the situation. Neil turns the volume to mute with the remote.

Neil That was quick. How'd it go? Alright?

Alex comes further into the room as Vicky and Neil have a brief staring competition.

Alex What's happened to my things?

Neil It's okay.

Alex What have you done with them?

Neil I haven't done anything. They're just packed away in the trunk.

Alex What for?

Neil To make room for my stuff. Give and take, Alex. You can't expect all the storage space.

Alex crosses to the trunk to check the contents. She throws a look towards Ray.

Alex What are you doing here?

Neil He's come to watch the game.

Alex starts checking the trunk as Vicky puts her bags down and takes off her coat.

(*to Alex*) So, was this it then? Who you were meeting? What's the big secret about that? (*Laughs. To Vicky*) She wouldn't tell me who it was. Bit adolescent, isn't it? (*Beat.*) How's Matty? Love's dream still blooming, is it?

Vicky just stares at him. Alex shuts the lid of the trunk and moves towards Ray.

Alex You came all the way over here to watch the game, did you?

Neil That's right.

Alex I'm not asking you. (*to Ray*) What else has he done?

She heads off into the bedroom to investigate, not waiting for an answer. Awkward beat. Ray is aware of Vicky's gaze. He smiles/nods. Her response is not encouraging. Ray looks/gestures to Neil for an intro-duction: he's quite impressed with her.

Neil Vicky. This is Splodge. Splodge. Vicky.

Ray Vicky . . .?

Neil Alex's sister.

Ray Hi. Nice to meet you.

Vicky blanks him. Alex returns, carrying one of the two suitcases.

Alex Where were you going to take these?

Neil What?

Alex (*to Ray*) Oxfam, maybe? Or just the local skip?

Neil You're getting paranoid. It's much simpler than that.

Alex Tell me.

Neil I'll need space for my clothes, won't I? I've been living out of a suitcase for the last few months, so I thought it was only fair that you took a turn –

Alex (*to Ray*) What was he really going to do with them?

Neil I've just said –

Alex (*flaring*) He can talk, can't he? (*to Ray*) Or do you need his permission for that now, along with everything else?

Neil (*laughs*) Well, answer her, Splodge.

Ray He asked me over to watch the game.

Alex He asked you here? To my flat? And you didn't think that was just a little bit odd?

Ray He said you'd got back together.

Alex He lied.

Neil He knows.

Ray Yeah, now I do.

Alex D'you know what I'd be thinking, Splodge? I'd be thinking, 'Christ, I'd better get out of here before it all turns *really* nasty.' But then that's just me.

Ray No, it's me an' all.

Alex (*beat*) Off you go, then.

Ray edges round the two women to approach Neil who's watching TV.

Neil Game's not over yet.

Ray No, I know but . . . I better . . . You know? Things to do . . .

Neil I'll see you later then.

Ray Yeah. Okay. Cheers. (*Mutters.*) Keys.

Neil looks up as Ray nudges him and furtively mimes his requirements.

Neil Yes, I've got them, thanks. (*to Alex*) That's the other reason he came round. He's going to lend me his van so I can move my stuff in.

Ray Eh?

Neil gets up and starts to guide a stunned Ray firmly towards the door. Alex moves to the TV set to switch it off.

Neil It's okay. I'll drop it round when I've finished – be tomorrow evening sometime.

They start to speak in muttered tones as Neil propels him to the door.

Ray No, I need it for tomorrow. For the match.

Neil You don't play any more –

Ray I'm still transport, ain't I? I've got to pick everyone up at the clubhouse. Nine o'clock.

Neil I can be there for nine.

Ray You ain't driving me van. You ain't insured.

Neil Neither are you.

Ray No, I know but . . .

Neil Trust me, alright? Here.

Ray What?

Neil It's your bus fare. I can't let you walk back, can I? Thanks mate.

Alex Splodge?

Ray (*normal voice*) Yeah, I'll see you around, Alex. Vicky.

Alex If my stuff goes missing – expect the police, won't you?

Ray gives a weak, feeble laugh as Neil pushes him out the door.

Neil Tomorrow at nine. Mind your knee.

Ray It's worth a taxi, innit?

Neil closes the door on his still-protesting face. Neil takes a beat, then comes back into the room to see the two women standing, waiting.

Neil Sorry about that. Just can't get the staff nowadays.

He laughs. They don't. Hostile face off.

Who's first?

Vicky Do you have any –

Alex I am.

Alex gives her sister a 'back-off' look then crosses to her bag.

I stopped in at the estate agents on the way back.

Neil Oh, yes?

Alex Yes. (*Beat.*) You can't sell this flat without my permission.

Neil Then give it.

Alex Here.

She offers him a form from her bag. He doesn't take it.

Neil What is it?

Alex Mortgage transfer. You should recognise it by now. I've sent you enough of them. I've marked where you need to sign.

Neil takes it and rips it in half. Alex pulls out a number of identical forms.

It's okay. I brought some spares.

Neil (*laughs. To Vicky*) Your turn.

Alex I haven't finished –

Neil I'm not giving you the flat, Alex. It's as simple as that.

Alex You promised –

Neil Oh, spare me the moral obligation lecture, please. I'm not interested. Okay?

Neil No, it's not okay –

Alex I don't care about guilt or conscience and neither will the courts. All they'll care about are the facts. It's a joint mortgage. It's legally half mine and there's nothing you can do about it. So let's stop pissing about and make the deal. Three options. One. We sell the flat, split the proceeds.

Alex No.

Vicky Why not?

Alex Because it's mine, that's why. I found this place. I put the deposit down. I'm paying the mortgage –

Neil I paid it too –

Alex You paid rent, Neil. You weren't investing in anything.

Vicky Second option?

Neil We share the flat. (*Gestures.*) Your bedroom, my bedroom. See how long it takes before one of us –

Alex What's the third?

Neil You buy me out.

Alex I've thought of a fourth. You have a road accident. You die horribly, writhing in the most unimaginable pain. The insurance pays off the mortgage. I live debt free. Everything's great.

Neil (*laughs*) Tempting, isn't it?

A stand-off. Vicky waits to see if Alex has any come-back. She doesn't.

Vicky (*to Neil*) How much?

Neil What?

Vicky To buy you out. Hypothetically. How much would you want?

Alex I'm not paying him anything.

Vicky I said, hypothetically. Neil?

Neil Thirty thousand.

Alex What?

Neil I know, I'm robbing myself but that's sentimentality for you.

Alex Thirty thousand pounds?

Neil It's worth seventy, isn't it?

Alex If we sold this property we'd make five thousand, tops.

Neil More than that.

Vicky She'd want the deposit back first. It was hers after all.

Neil If you say so.

Alex Which means, after fees, we'd have about two thousand each. Probably less.

Neil You want to buy my half for two grand?

Alex I don't need to buy it at all. I've already paid, Neil. Every night you were off screwing your boss.

Neil Her name's Caroline.

Alex Must be awkward now it's over. I hope it's not going to affect your job or anything.

Neil fights to keep his self-control. He laughs, a little forced.

Neil Are you finished?

Vicky No. If I write you a cheque for five thousand pounds, will you sign the transfer?

Alex What? What?

Neil You mean, hypothetically?

Vicky No, I mean really. I can write it out now if you like.

Vicky moves to get her cheque-book and pen.

Alex Don't. Vicky. What do you think you're doing?

Vicky Helping.

Alex I didn't ask you for this. I said, to keep out of it.

Vicky (*to Neil*) It's Ryder with a 'y', yes?

Alex It's got nothing to do with you.

Vicky If you can think of an alternative solution, Alex, then fine – let's hear it.

Alex I don't want –

Vicky Of course, getting him to sign the form eight months ago would have been the most intelligent option.

Alex Oh, that's right. Perfect. Make this my fault.

Vicky (*writing*) Five thousand pounds.

Alex For Christ's sake. Don't you get what he's doing? It's not about the money. That's not what he wants. (*to Neil*) Is it? Tell her.

Alex and Neil stare at eachother while Vicky finishes writing the cheque. Vicky tears it off and holds it out for him. Beat. Neil takes the cheque. Alex laughs/ scoffs, puts the transfer forms down and collects up the shopping bags. She moves off towards the bedroom, bundling open the door.

(*to Neil*) She'll go to ten if you push her.

Vicky I don't think so.

Alex goes into the bedroom and closes the door. Vicky puts her cheque-book away and moves to pick up one of the transfer forms. Neil moves to the coffee table to take a swig of lager.

You've got to sign this.

Neil Next Friday, yes.

Vicky What?

Neil I'll put the cheque in Monday. Three working days to clear. Next Friday – if it's still there – I'll sign the form.

Vicky I promise you it won't bounce.

Neil I promised her this flat.

A stand-off. Vicky blinks first.

Vicky Alright, I'll have my solicitor draw up a proper agreement.

Neil What for?

Vicky Because I'll need a guarantee that –

Neil I told you. Once the cheque clears, I'll sign.

Vicky Once it's cleared, you won't have to.

Neil (*laughs*) You see, this is the value of thinking things through. What's Matty going to say when he finds out you've just gifted me five big ones? That's if he notices – the amount you get through.

Neil rips the cheque into quarters and tosses it towards her, dismissive.

Didn't achieve much, did it? Aside from humiliating your sister, of course – always a plus in your eyes, let's face it.

Vicky It's a genuine offer. I can phone my solicitor –

Neil You are so far out of your depth I'm frightened for you.

Vicky No, you're just frightened, Neil. What happened? Things get a bit fucked-up? Thought you'd come crawling back to the womb?

Neil (*laughs*) That's right. Crowded, isn't it?

Vicky Last chance.

Neil You can't help her with money, Vicky. You can't hurt her with it either. What else have you got?

A stand-off. They stare malevolently at each other for a beat. Vicky smiles/laughs, biding her time. She returns the form to the pile, picks up her bag and heads for the bedroom.

I'd say your sister deserves an apology. Wouldn't you?

Vicky turns at the door, giving him a final look.

Vicky You should've taken the money, Neil. I'm going to enjoy watching you realise that.

She knocks on the bedroom door and enters, closing the door behind her. Neil takes another swig of lager, brooding, unsettled by her confidence. Fade to black.

SCENE THREE

Evening. Neil is standing by the window, staring at the outside world: it is raining. The TV is off and the lights have been turned low on the dimmer switch. Alex exits from the bedroom in a larger size version of the black dress she took back to the shops. Neil turns, watching as she moves to the kitchen and takes a bottle of wine from the fridge. She takes two wine glasses from the cupboard, a corkscrew from the drawer and starts to open a bottle.

Neil Looks good. The dress.

Alex Thank you.

Neil They let you change it then?

Alex Yes. I got one with a zip that worked.

Neil (*laughs*) You should have told him your real size. You'll have to take back everything he gets you now.

Neil looks back out the window. Alex works on opening the wine.

'Shiny Eric's' has gone. When'd that happen?

Alex What?

Neil The snooker hall. It's all boarded up.

Alex I don't know.

Neil 'S a fuck. I used to get all our blow from there.

Alex works the cork out and starts to pour two glasses of wine. Neil starts fiddling with the catch, trying to open the window.

Alex It's stuck. Leave it.

Neil I want to feel the rain, get some air.

Alex Well, go outside then. (*off his look*) I'll let you back in.

They smile. She puts the bottle back in the fridge and picks up the two glasses of wine.

Neil Why don't we both go out? Get up on the roof? Do a bit of . . . *au naturel.*

Neil does a little salsa-like shimmy, pouting. Alex laughs at the reminder of a happier past event. She approaches with the wine.

Alex Here.

He's surprised, assuming it was for her sister, but takes it automatically.

Put some music on if you like.

She moves to the bedroom and goes in. Neil deliberates for a moment, then goes to the trunk to select a CD. Alex returns, carrying a make-up bag and a mirror. She moves to the dimmer switch, turns the lights up to full, then moves to the sofa. She sits and starts to apply her make-up. Neil has selected a CD and moves to the stereo unit. He puts it on: a soulful, mellow tune that holds strong personal memories for them both. She looks up at him briefly when it starts then carries on with her make-up. Neil sips his wine, watching her.

Neil You not having any?

Alex I'll share yours.

Beat. Alex carries on with her make-up. Neil watches her, a bit thrown by her tactics.

Neil She down for the weekend then? The Duchess.

Alex That's right. We're going to go and see Mum tomorrow.

Neil How's she doing?

Alex (*grimaces*) Hard to tell. She's out of her Sylvia Plath phase and moving towards a more Borgia mentality.

Neil (*laughs*) What about your Dad?

Alex Oh, he's just peachy – can't see what all the fuss is about.

Neil Don't put too much of that on.

Alex I won't. (*Corrects herself.*) I'll do what I like, okay?

Neil He's the same as me. Finds too much a real turn-off.

Alex gives him a look, thinks about saying something, doesn't. She resumes her work.

Alex What are you planning for tonight?

Neil Why?

Alex I want to know what to expect when we get back.

Neil Are you bringing him here?

Alex I meant, me and Vicky. We're not going to find you in bed with some tragic female?

Neil I wouldn't. Not here.

Alex Make a difference, does it?

Neil I've never brought anyone here.

Alex looks at him sharply – Caroline?

No.

They look at each other for a longer beat than Alex intended. She resumes her work, stops. She puts her make-up down and starts to refasten her suspender strap which has unaccountably come loose. She takes her time, knowing Neil is watching her. She flicks a glance at him as she resumes her make-up.

Alex I thought stockings rather than tights. What do you think?

Neil smiles, knowing it was deliberate.

Neil Why not? Bit tarty, but –

Alex He likes tarty.

Neil Obviously.

Alex I like doing what he likes. (*Beat. Laughs.*) It's funny that, isn't it? You meet a certain person and suddenly, you'll do things, and let him do things, that you point-blank refused to do with your other boyfriends. With them it was a problem. But with this person . . . it's great.

Neil struggles to hide how much that's got to him, fails.

Did you find that? With Caroline?

Neil (*beat*) Absolutely.

Alex smiles and resumes her work.

Alex How difficult, is it? In the office.

Neil I don't work there any more.

Alex She got you fired?

Neil Subtler than that. She's drafted me onto a new project, supposedly to sort out all the kinks in the program, only the software's in a language I don't quite understand.

Alex I'm impressed. You must have really fucked her off.

Neil It's a special talent I have.

Alex What went wrong?

Neil Nothing. Same as us, I suppose. After a while you just want something different.

Alex I didn't want something different.

Neil Something more.

Alex Something extra, you mean.

Vicky (*off*) Oohhh. (*Calls.*) Alex?

Alex What?

Vicky (*off*) I've dropped a contact. It's on your desk somewhere.

Alex puts her stuff down, exasperated. She gets up.

(*off*) Alex? I can't find it. I can't see, can I? Alex?

Alex Yes, alright. I'm coming.

Vicky (*off*) 'S okay, I've got it. 'S okay.

Alex exchanges a look with Neil and sits back down. He offers her the glass of wine. She smiles gratefully

and takes a much-needed sip. She keeps hold of it,
brooding.

Neil Are you nervous?

She puts the glass down and picks up the mirror to
check her handiwork.

Alex No. Why?

Neil What if they don't get on?

Alex Everyone gets on with Ben, Neil. You know that.

She makes a few final touches then poses for him. He
nods approvingly.

Too much?

Neil Just right.

She continues anyway, just to make a point. Neil
finishes the wine and gets up to go for a refill.

Where are you meeting him?

Alex Soho.

Neil Anywhere particular?

Alex Tapas bar. (*off his look*) Not that one.

Neil Right.

Alex I'm not sure where we'll eat yet but I can let you
have a full itinerary tomorrow.

Neil Are you going to tell him I'm here?

Alex I'm hoping the evening won't be that dull.

Neil Maybe you should. I expect your version's a lot
safer than mine.

Alex What's your version?

Neil I came round. We talked. Slept together.

Alex (*laughs*) Was I pathetically grateful?

Neil I think you might have been, yes.

Alex Anything else?

Neil Only that at one point you said how great it was not to have to fake it any more.

Alex (*laughs*) No, I've said that one to him already.

> *Neil didn't like that. He replaces the wine in the fridge and comes back over. Alex has started to pack away her make-up.*

Neil 'Course, I could just say I spent the night. And smile. Let him imagine the rest. That's what I did with Splodge.

Alex Did it work?

Neil Oh, yes. He had us 'fucking like dogs' on the sofa. (*Laughs.*) I don't want to disturb you but I think you feature quite heavily in his masturbation fantasies.

Alex (*beat*) He asked me out once.

Neil When?

Alex Way back. Just after you'd gone. I came home one day to find a card and a rose by the door. It said if I ever wanted someone to trust, who'd never, ever, cheat on me, then to call this number.

Neil This is Splodge we're talking about?

Alex I'm sure it was him. I used to see him around all the time. I thought he was stalking me at first.

Neil (*laughs*) Did you call the number?

Alex No.

Neil Why not? It might have been someone else.

Alex I didn't want anyone else.

A moment between them. Neil leans forward reaching out with his hand. She pulls back.

What?

Neil It's okay. You've got an eyelash. Here.

He delicately takes her eyelash and places it on his finger, holding it up for her to blow.

Make a wish.

She thinks, makes a wish, and blows at the eyelash. Neil clutches his heart and falls, faking a good, comic death throe. She laughs. Vicky exits from the bedroom, all dressed up in full attack mode. She's carrying her empty glass and handbag. She registers the mood between the others but pretends to ignore it.

Vicky It's five-to.

Alex I know.

Vicky What do you think?

She does a little pose: she looks great, far better than Alex. They all know it.

Alex Yes. It's nice.

Vicky It's okay, isn't it? Not too . . .

Alex What?

Vicky I don't know. Well, as long as you like it. I want to make a good impression.

Vicky heads for the fridge. Neil looks at Alex, who has fallen a little thoughtful at her sister's appearance.

Vicky Is there any wine left?

Neil Chucking it back a bit, aren't you?

Vicky Alex? Is it in the fridge?

She gets the bottle out the fridge and helps herself to another glass.

Neil I suppose you need to get a bit psyched up, don't you? So you can make that fake little speech of yours.

Vicky (*to Alex*) Did you want some?

Alex What speech?

Vicky I'll finish it, shall I?

Neil (*to Alex*) She waits 'til you've gone to the loo then gives out this big 'if you hurt my sister, I'll cut your bollocks off' number. (*Laughs. To Vicky*) I don't think it works somehow. Do you?

Vicky It's too early to say. She hasn't been out with anyone who had a pair yet.

Alex laughs and heads off to the bedroom to put her make-up back. Vicky is pleased at her sister's reaction. She sips at her wine as Neil gets out his cigarettes.

Can't you wait 'til we've gone?

He lights it, blowing the smoke in her general direction.

Neil Good feeling, is it?

Vicky Sorry?

Neil What you're doing.

Vicky I don't know what you're talking about.

Neil You're quite a little cunt in your own way, aren't you?

Vicky (*beat*) Is that meant to be intimidating?

Neil I'm just stating a fact.

Vicky It's okay, Neil. If you want to abuse me, go ahead. I know how frustrated you must feel.

Neil About what exactly?

Vicky Your mediocrity. I hear Ben's really quite something.

Neil Compared to Matty, yes. I think he probably is.

Vicky (*smiles*) Don't wait up, will you?

The toilet flushes. Vicky drains her glass and moves towards the front door to get the coats.

Vicky (*calling*) Are you ready, Alex?

Alex (*off*) Coming.

Alex comes out of the bedroom. Vicky comes across and hands her her coat.

Vicky You look great.

Alex Yes?

Vicky Yes. Really good.

Neil laughs. Vicky glares at him. Alex looks round, paranoid.

Alex What?

Neil I'm laughing at her. Not you.

Vicky He's being a prick. Let's go.

Vicky goes. Alex moves to follow.

Neil Alex? (*Beat.*) Have fun.

Alex Thanks.

Vicky (*off*) Alex?

Alex Bye.

She smiles and goes. Neil gives her a sort of smile/ wave as she closes the door. He moves to the kitchen and searches through the drawers. He finds a screw- driver and takes it to the bedroom. He starts to unscrew the lock on the bedroom door. Fade to black.

SCENE FOUR

Night. Neil is on the sofa, sifting through one of the suitcases of Alex's clothes. He picks out a small summer dress, a particular favourite: the first thing he ever saw her wearing. He rummages further, finding an old T-shirt. He takes off his own shirt and puts the T-shirt on instead. He rummages further, starting as he hears a key in the lock. He puts the panties and dress back in the suitcase, shoving it aside. He feigns a nonchalant 'slouch with magazine' pose as Vicky comes in – she's drunk and upset but hiding it quite successfully. Neil puts the magazine down and sits up. Vicky takes off her coat and hangs it up.

Neil Where's Alex?

Vicky I don't know. Where does Ben live?

Neil She's staying with him?

Vicky moves over to kitchen, taking her handbag with her. Neil gets up to follow.

She said she was coming back here.

Vicky Changed her mind.

Neil How come?

Vicky (*laughs*) No wonder you feel so inadequate.

She puts her bag on the unit top, switches the kettle on and starts to make herself a coffee in a noisy, careless fashion. Neil watches her, thinking it through.

Neil What was it about?

Vicky What?

Neil The argument.

Vicky There wasn't an –

Neil You've pissed her off, Vicky. You must have done. That's the only reason she would've –

Vicky Listen, you sad little residue. We've had a wonderful night. We didn't fight or argue, we just talked, ate great seafood and drank champagne. It was terrific. Ben is everything you're not and she wanted to have sex with him. Get over it.

She has reached into her bag and got out a packet of cigarettes. She lights one with none too steady hands. Neil smiles.

Neil Not as easy as you thought, was it?

Vicky takes a deep drag and exhales, studying Neil thoughtfully.

Vicky What are you doing here? What do you want? Really?

Neil The same as you.

Vicky (*beat. Smiles. Wry*) Yes.

She takes another drag and looks at her watch, then takes her mobile phone out of the bag. She starts to dial. Neil helps himself to one of her cigarettes.

Neil Checking in?

Vicky They like each other a lot, Neil. They're good together.

Neil I know.

Neil lights his cigarette and heads off into the bedroom. Vicky gets the ansaphone, waits to leave a message. Neil reappears with a blanket and sheet as she speaks, standing in the doorway, listening.

Vicky Hi, it's me. It's about eleven-thirty. I'm back, safe. We've had a lovely time. Alex is looking great, her boyfriend's very nice, so no worries there. She's really traded up for once, thank goodness. I'll tell you all about it tomorrow. Love you. Hope Susie settled okay. I love you both. Bye.

She puts her phone down and moves to the fridge to get some milk.

Neil That was beautiful.

She gives him a look. He grins and moves to dump the bed stuff on the sofa.

Doesn't it bother you? Saturday night. Still not back.

Vicky He's not out. He's in bed.

Neil Interesting man.

Vicky Responsible, yes. He's been looking after Susie.

Neil Well, she won't have any trouble sleeping then. I always felt myself going after five minutes – if she's had to spend the whole evening with him. (*Laughs.*) How do you manage it? I suppose the money compensates.

Vicky I don't find my husband boring.

Neil It's a fuck that, isn't it? Compromising to get what you want.

Vicky I didn't.

Neil Then realising what you gave up seems so much more worthwhile.

Vicky I didn't compromise.

Neil It's okay, he'll probably leave you soon. Let's face it, it's a good bet, isn't it? Your father fucked off, I messed up Alex – can you see a sort of pattern emerging?

Vicky smiles, tight-lipped, trying to control her anger at his taunts.

Vicky Well, you know all about people leaving, don't you Neil? I wonder what Caroline's doing tonight? Fucking someone else, probably – same as Alex. D'you see a pattern emerging in that?

Neil (*laughs*) Touched a nerve, didn't it?

Vicky They've moved on. You're the one going back-wards, squatting on a sofa, trying to –

Neil No, I'm sleeping in there tonight. This is *your* bed, Vicky. You're okay with that, aren't you?

Vicky (*beat*) Fine.

Neil I'll leave the door open, of course, in case you want to come in.

Vicky Don't flatter yourself.

Neil Even royalty have to piss, Duchess. What did you think I meant?

The kettle has boiled. Vicky smiles/scoffs and turns away to start making her coffee.

No, really. I'm interested. What?

Vicky You tell me.

Neil I'm not a fucking telepath. 'Don't flatter yourself'? What's that implying?

Vicky stirs her cup and turns to face him.

Vicky I don't know, Neil. You're the one who's interested. What would you like it to imply?

A stand-off. Neil smiles – they know exactly where they're at.

Neil Cheat on Matt a lot, do you?

Vicky Say it.

Neil What about Ben?

Vicky What?

Neil Did you show Alex you could? Is that what the argument was about?

Vicky We didn't argue –

Neil You'd like to fuck him though, wouldn't you?

Vicky I don't know, Neil. Would you?

Neil (*laughs*) Is that what he said?

Vicky No, I think his actual words were 'I'm going to punch his fucked-up little head in.'

Neil Who told him I was here?

Vicky She did. It was the first thing she said. She's completely open with him. She doesn't want you to start messing it up.

Neil You have no idea what she wants.

Vicky I thought we were discussing what you wanted.

Neil That's not what we were doing.

Vicky Come on, Neil. Don't bottle it now. What's it going to take? It's not money, right? So, what is it? What else do you want?

Neil (*beat*) I'll get it from Alex if you don't mind. Yours smells rancid enough from here.

He laughs mockingly at her. Vicky struggles to restrain her hatred.

Vicky Don't you dare hurt my sister.

Neil I think your therapist'd call that 'transference'.

Vicky (*flaring*) Don't you fucking dare!

Neil There's plenty for everyone, Vicky.

Vicky Don't.

Neil You'll get your share.

Vicky She's with Ben.

Neil She might be bouncing up and down on top of him but that's not what we're talking about, is it?

Vicky It's over.

Neil She won't sell this flat. She knows I'll stay and yet she still won't. What's Ben saying about that, eh? Does he even know?

Vicky is caught at that. Neil presses his advantage.

She's got my photo in her purse. Eight months. And it's still my photo. Mine. Not Ben's. She asked me to stay. Last night. I was going to go and she offered me blankets and –

Vicky I said, don't.

Neil Or what? You can yap about it all you like but in the end what the fucking hell are you going to do? Cut my balls off? Well, go on then.

Vicky She's pregnant.

Neil didn't expect that. Vicky lets it sink right in before the follow-up.

Three months. It's Ben's. Hope that didn't hurt too much.

Vicky heads off towards the bedroom.

Neil I don't believe you.

Vicky I'm going to use the bathroom now. Okay? Save disturbing you later.

Neil She would've said.

Vicky Why would she? It's none of your business.

Neil Yes, it is.

Vicky No. It isn't. You're not a part of her life, Neil. You're just something she stepped in. Still clinging to her shoes.

She moves into the bedroom, closing the bedroom door. Neil stands there, shell-shocked.

Fade to black.

Act Two (Sunday)

SCENE ONE

Morning. The trunk and the suitcase are still there. Vicky sits on the sofa, nursing a mug of coffee, brooding. She is wearing Alex's silk dressing gown. A blanket and sheet lie rumpled next to her. Her mobile phone and cigarettes are on the table. She takes a sip of coffee, puts the mug down and lights herself a cigarette, checking to see how many are left in the packet: not enough. She tosses it down and picks up her mobile, dials. She stands up as she waits for a connection.

Vicky Hi. Matty? It's me. Yes, I'm fine. What happened to you? Last night. I called, didn't you get the message? About half-eleven. Where the hell were you? I see. What about Susie? Well, who was looking after her? What are you doing, letting a fifteen-year-old babysit 'til one am? She could've picked up the phone – let me know everything was alright – well, how the fuck would you feel if I decided to . . .

He's hung up. Vicky curses silently. She takes a deep drag of her cigarette and dials again, waits.

Matthew, pick up the phone. I'm sorry, okay? I was worried. I didn't mean to . . . (*He picks up.*) Hi. Look, I'm sorry. Yes, I know. No, it's not that . . . You didn't mention it beforehand, that's all. Yes. Okay. Fine. Alright. Let's just forget about it. Is Susie there? Well, can you tell her I phoned? Say I'll be back this evening. I don't know yet. We're going over to Mum's for lunch. Which'll be nice.

The intercom buzzer sounds. Vicky looks round and starts to move towards it.

Can I phone you from the station when I get in? I'll get a cab then, shall I? Right. Fine. Enjoy your golf.

She ends the call. The buzzer is sounding repeatedly. Vicky presses the intercom switch.

Hello? Who is it?

Alex (*off*) It's me. Open the door.

Vicky presses the door release and leaves the door to the flat ajar. She takes a final pull on the cigarette then moves to the sink to stub it out. She throws the butt away in the bin and waves half-heartedly around to dissipate the smoke. She moves to the window and struggles to open it but it's jammed tight. She gives it up and moves to the kettle to flick it on. She collects her mug and starts making coffee for them both. Alex enters, carrying a Sunday newspaper and a pint of milk. She shuts the door with a healthy bang and strides over to the kitchen unit to dump her paper and milk.

Vicky Morning.

Alex gives her a black look as she takes off her coat, returning to the door to hang it up. She is still wearing her dress from the night before.

I'm making coffee. D'you want some?

Alex Where's Neil?

Vicky Out.

Alex Where?

Vicky I don't know. It was before I got up.

Alex sees Vicky flicking through her paper. She moves across to snatch it off her.

What are you doing?

Alex It's mine. Get your own if you want one.

Vicky I can read a bit of it, surely?

Alex I haven't decided what part I want yet.

Vicky Well, let me know and we'll swap.

Vicky tries to take a section but Alex swats her hand away.

Don't be stupid.

Alex Are you still smoking?

Vicky Just using up the pack.

Alex Don't smoke in my flat.

Vicky That's Neil's prerogative, is it?

Alex I knew you'd start again.

Vicky It's not my fault. Your boyfriend started me off.

Alex With a little persuasion, yes. 'Oh, Ben – can I have a puff? Oh, this is awful, I've been ever so good 'til now.'

Vicky I didn't say it like that.

Alex No, yours had a more retard quality, but then you practice it more often than I do.

Vicky It was just fun, that's all.

Alex looks at her, trying to repress an impending explosion.

Alex That's right. Good 'fun', wasn't it?

She moves to the sofa, shoves the blanket and sheet out of the way, irritated.

Wouldn't have occurred to you to fold these, I suppose?

She sits and opens her paper, staring at it without reading a word. Vicky shrugs and moves to the kitchen to carry on with the coffee. Alex puts the paper down, even more irritated, and stands to fold the sheet and blanket herself.

Alex You're wearing my dressing gown.

Vicky So?

Alex So it'll stink of smoke now, won't it?

Vicky I'll have it dry-cleaned.

Alex Yes, or just buy me a new one, eh? I mean, why not? It's not like it costs you anything.

Vicky I'm assuming there's a point to all this.

Alex stops folding the blanket, debating whether to have it out. She resumes folding the blanket. Vicky decides she wants to push it.

Ben smoked – I had a relapse – what's the big deal? We're the ones who'll get cancer.

Alex Yes, you and him, right? 'We're the ones'. You always find it, don't you?

Vicky What?

Alex That 'thing' that lets you get all exclusive with my boyfriends – something I don't do or aren't interested in –

Vicky Like smoking?

Alex Like that scuba-diving crap. When were you ever interested in that? 'Oh yes, I'd love to do that.' You hate the bloody water –

Vicky No, I don't –

Alex It's messes up your perfect fucking hair for a start.

Vicky It's not perfect.

Alex And why do you have to 'touch' people all the time? Every time he made you laugh, you gave his arm a little touch, pawing away at it, leaving it there just a little bit longer each time –

Vicky No, I wasn't –

Alex Making sure he noticed.

Vicky What are you getting so insecure about? You're the one he went home with.

Alex Yes, I was, wasn't I?

Vicky Yes.

Alex Yes.

Alex tucks the folded sheet and blanket under her arm and collects up the paper before heading for the bedroom.

That's right. And you'd better remember that next time. If there is a next time which I seriously doubt.

Vicky Why, what happened?

Alex Oh, don't get your hopes up. We're fine, no thanks to you –

Vicky I don't fancy him if that's what you're worried about.

Alex That's not why you do it.

A stand-off. Vicky laughs.

Vicky Okay, look – I'll back off a bit. You keep him hidden 'til you feel a bit more secure then –

Alex throws the paper at her face. Vicky is shocked at her action.

Alex You wanted to read it, didn't you? Pick a section. I'm going to get changed.

Alex stomps off into the bedroom with the sheet and blanket. Vicky takes a beat, then bends down and starts to pick up the scattered newspaper.

Vicky (*calls*) I'm sorry. Okay? Alex? I just . . . It's just the way I am with people. I wanted him to like me. It was important. Especially after Neil.

Alex (*off*) Yes, I can see that.

Vicky I liked him. He's not my type but I thought he was great. Really good fun. Good job. Good body.

Alex (*off*) Well, you touched enough of it.

Vicky I thought you were really lucky. I was proud of you.

Alex (*off*) Stunned, you mean.

Vicky (*to self*) Yep.

Silence. Vicky puts the paper on the table. She moves to the bedroom doorway.

So, how did it go? D'you get everything straightened out?

Alex (*off*) What did Neil say when you got back?

Vicky Not a lot. (*Beat.*) He was on the phone to some other girl. Something called Lucy, I think. I don't know. Probably a sex line – he put it down pretty quickly when I came in.

Alex (*off*) What about the fact I wasn't with you?

Vicky Well, that's probably why he's gone, isn't it? Made him realise what a prick he's been. Don't you think?

Alex (*off*) What's happened to the lock?

Vicky What?

Alex comes out in slob gear: tracksuit pants and sweat-shirt. She examines the door.

Alex I put a lock here. A bolt. He must have taken it off.

Vicky looks at her blankly.

Neil. Last night when we were out. Didn't you notice?

Vicky No.

Alex You didn't lock the door?

Vicky No. Why?

Alex When you went to bed. Why not?

Vicky I didn't sleep in there. He did. I was on that all night.

Alex takes a beat to think through the implications.

Alex Keys. You've still got them, haven't you?

Vicky What?

Alex To the flat. The keys –

Vicky Yes. They're in my bag.

Alex Show me.

Vicky What?

Alex Where is it?

She looks around, spots Vicky's handbag. She picks it up, starting to search through it.

Vicky I'll do it. Don't poke around in my bag.

Alex They're not there.

Alex tosses the bag to Vicky who makes her own futile search.

That's why he's not here, isn't it? That's great, Vicky. Thanks.

Vicky It's not my fault.

Alex I told you not to let him get them.

Vicky What was I supposed to do? Stay awake all night, guarding them?

Alex You could've hidden them.

Vicky I didn't think. I was pissed.

Alex For Christ's sake –

Vicky You should've come back with me. Both of you.

Alex Oh, yes. Fabulous idea. You saw what Ben was like when he knew Neil was here.

Vicky Why do you think I told him?

Alex I know exactly why you told him.

Vicky If you'd let him come round, this would all be over by now. He could have punched Neil's head in, made him sign the lease, then kicked him out. And you'd be saying, 'Thanks Vicky, I should listen to you more often.'

Alex Or alternatively, Neil would be in hospital, Ben would be up on some assault charge –

Vicky They wouldn't charge him. It'd be our word against Neil's. Three against one.

Alex If you'd spent the night at Mum's like I said –

Vicky I didn't want to –

Alex Why not?

Vicky I thought at least one of us should be here. Keep an eye on the flat.

Alex That's not the reason.

Vicky Make sure Neil wasn't wrecking it.

Alex You just didn't want to have to listen to her telling you all about what a cunt our father really is.

Vicky No –

Alex No, you've kept well out of that one, haven't you? All the dirty details that might ruin your image of Daddy.

Vicky I visit her. I do my bit.

Alex She doesn't think so.

Vicky You don't keep in contact with Dad.

Alex I won't go on holiday with him and that thing, that's for sure.

Vicky Well, that's very mature of you.

Alex Yes, I just childishly mopped up the bathroom when our Mum cut her arms to pieces. If only I'd been more adult I could've gone skiing with the people who caused it.

Vicky You could've come. I'd have paid for you. I said that.

Alex laughs/scoffs at that.

What? He fell in love with someone else – that's all.

Alex You haven't listened to Mum's side. I don't think forcing someone to have anal sex –

Vicky Stop it –

Alex In the six months before he left he did everything he could –

Vicky I don't want to know –

Alex To hurt and humiliate her. And she let him. She thought she had to. Because otherwise he'd leave her. No, I don't keep in contact. Sorry.

Vicky takes a beat on that. She regroups.

Vicky But you'll let Neil stay the night? After everything he did –

Alex I didn't let him in to stay. I told you. He was drunk.

Vicky And upset, yes, I know. How fucking altruistic –

Alex He said, he wanted to talk.

Vicky About what? What could he possibly have to say that you wanted to hear?

A stand-off. They both know the answer, both waiting for the other to say it.

Vicky You said it wasn't the money. That he wanted. So what did you think it was? What were you hoping it was? That he'd come back?

Alex Yes.

Vicky Thank you.

Alex I just wanted to hear him say it. That's all.

Vicky Right.

Alex Ask if he could. I wanted to listen to him apologise and admit that yes, he'd made a big mistake – that I was the person he wanted. Needed. I was going to make him beg and humiliate himself and go through all the shitty pleading he forced me through so I could have the pleasure of kicking his guts out – make him know what it was like, what it had felt like, still feels like, for me.

Beat. Vicky gauges the explanation, Alex's emotional state.

Vicky That's not what you'd have done.

Alex (*beat*) Well, that's your opinion, isn't it?

Vicky Alex. You carry his photo around with you.

Alex What?

Vicky You've got his photo in your purse. He told me.

Alex (*beat*) No.

Alex goes to get her purse and sift through the contents. She brings the photo out.

I didn't know.

Vicky Okay.

Alex I didn't know. If I'd known I'd have gotten rid of it. (*Beat.*) He's not what I want.

Vicky Prove it.

Alex rips the photo up. Vicky laughs.

What about a slightly bigger statement? What about selling the flat?

Alex I'm going to. Tomorrow. Ben said it was that or he'd walk and I believed him.

Vicky is taken aback by that.

Vicky Oh, right.

Alex Why? What's wrong? What have you done?

Vicky Nothing.

Alex What have you said? (*Beat.*) He knows, doesn't he? About me. You told him.

Vicky He'd have found out sooner or later.

Alex From me, yes.

Vicky What's it matter?

Alex You promised me you wouldn't say. Vicky –

Vicky The point is, surely, he knows. He knows you're not available. He knows it's over. He's not going to do anything – he's all talk. That's all he's ever been. What do you still see in him?

A stand-off. Alex studies her carefully.

Alex It never worked with Neil, did it? What you did last night. With Ben.

Vicky I didn't do anything –

Alex All my boyfriends – I'd watch you flirt and laugh and have them flirt right back while I sat there feeling dull and stupid and deeply unattractive –

Vicky Alex –

Alex I remember getting to the stage when I thought, well at least they won't chuck me because being with me means they get closer to you. 'Cos they were right. You were prettier, funnier – and every time you laughed at their jokes and then looked at me, like we were sharing something, I knew what you were doing was laughing at me, and saying, 'You see? I could take him anytime I wanted – I just don't want to.'

Vicky No.

Alex Only with Neil you couldn't. He wanted me. And I could see how scared that made you – that maybe what he thought about you was right. And that everyone else was wrong.

Vicky He doesn't scare me.

Alex You were so happy when we finished.

Vicky Because he's a shit.

Alex You had that look in your eyes that you always get when my relationships fuck up, or work goes badly –

and it's almost a kind of euphoria – or relief rather that yes, you are still better than me.

Vicky I've never thought that.

Alex It's why you told Ben about Neil being here. You saw something really good and did everything you could to ruin it.

Vicky and Alex try and stare each other down. Alex wins. Vicky gives a wry laugh. She moves to her bag and takes out a card, lays it on the unit top.

Vicky Here. I'd say you have some personal issues need exploring.

Alex I don't need a therapist, thank you.

Vicky No, this is so much more healthy, isn't it?

Alex Oh, for Christ's sake –

Vicky (*flaring*) Don't you dare fucking blame me for your inadequacies, Alex. I am sick of hearing how much the problems people have are down to me. *My* deficiencies. Well, I'm sorry I'm not quite what people wanted, or how they expected me to be, but then maybe I'm not so fucking thrilled with the situation either. That wouldn't occur to anyone though, would it? No, so much easier to interpret what I do as nothing more than self-obsessed shit. 'Cos, of course, I have no-one else's interests at heart. How could I? I'm too absorbed in my own neurotic compulsions to possibly contemplate what anyone else might want. I'm just a nasty little cunt, aren't I? That's all I've ever been – a nice to look at, selfish, bitter cunt.

Beat. Vicky moves to get a cigarette and calm herself down. Alex watches her, gauging her sister's outburst, emotional state.

You'd better add weak-willed to that list as well. I can go outside if you like.

Alex (*shrugs*) It's up to you.

Vicky takes a couple of defiant deep drags, awkward at Alex's scrutiny.

Vicky What time are we meeting Mum?

Alex One o'clock.

Vicky We should probably order a cab. Have you got a number?

Alex Somewhere, yes. I'll do it later.

Beat. Vicky stubs her cigarette out in the lid of the packet – a definite concession.

Alex Thank you.

Vicky (*going*) I need a shower.

Alex Vicky.

Vicky I won't be long.

Alex I'm not going.

Vicky (*turns*) What?

Alex To Mum's. I can't, can I? Not now Neil's got the keys.

Vicky You don't have a spare set?

Alex No.

Vicky (*beat. Laughs*) Well, I'll have to see her on my own then, won't I? Or maybe I'll just go back home. Get in some more quality time with my own family.

Alex (*beat*) It's okay then, is it? With Matt? Everything –

Vicky It's great. Really. We're fine. I spoke to him this morning. He sends his love, says he's really pleased things are working out.

Alex Right.

Vicky He's been getting at me a bit about your promotion. Thinks maybe I should do something similar. Start earning my keep.

Alex Might do you some good. Shouldn't be a problem. You got a better degree than me.

Vicky That's right. And you're a marketing 'manager' now. So what should I aspire to? Supervisor?

Alex bristles at her patronising tone/look.

Alex I *need* to work. You don't.

Vicky (*smiles. Beat*) You'll be alright then, will you? Just you and Neil?

Alex He's all talk, isn't he? I'll be fine.

Vicky goes into the bedroom and closes the door. Alex sits on the sofa, brooding.

SCENE TWO

Afternoon. Alex is in kitchen beginning to prepare her lunch: soup from a carton, fresh salad with a little dressing, organic bread with filling. Ray stands near the front door, still wearing his coat and scarf, feeling very awkward and uncomfortable. He watches as Alex takes some vegetables out of the fridge.

Ray I wouldn't have bothered you normally, it's just . . . he's got my van, see?

Alex gives him a look.

72

He was meant to pick us up at nine. Take us all over to Monk Hill for the game. Had to go by taxi in the end – cost a fortune. You don't know where he is, do you?

Alex No.

Ray I phoned here earlier. When we were all waiting. Your sister said he'd gone so I thought he must be on his way. Only he never showed.

Alex Maybe he's had an accident.

Ray No, don't say that. I need it for work, don't I?

Alex laughs. Ray is encouraged enough to come a little further into the room.

I've been round to his bedsit but he's not there either. I thought he might have come here. Start dropping off his stuff.

Alex Nope.

Ray Well, where the hell –

Alex I thought you wanted to apologise? For yesterday.

Ray Yeah, I do. I'm sorry.

Alex Is that it?

Ray Well, it's like I said, innit? I didn't know what was going on. He told me you'd got back together. Said he wanted to talk. Watch the match.

Alex Right.

Ray If I'd known he was lying, I wouldn't have come, would I? (*Beat.*) It was lucky I did, mind. It was me who stopped him. No way, I said. I ain't nicking her stuff.

Alex But here's the keys to my van so you can do it yourself.

Ray No, see, that was a trick, wasn't it? Before I knew what he was up to – I wouldn't have given them to him otherwise.

Alex Why not take them back? Once you knew.

Ray Well, I would've.

Alex Only?

Ray He was scared, weren't he?

Alex What?

Ray Yes. Of this Ben bloke. Reckoned he was a bit dangerous, you know? Said he'd feel safer if I was there – give him some back-up in case it got violent.

Alex laughs. Ray bristles a little at that.

What? I got a real temper when I get going. 'S how I crooked me knee in the first place. Big pub fight it was. Two blokes with pool cues. I took 'em out, single-handed – they still talk about it down the club.

Alex *(dry)* Really.

Ray 'S okay, I wouldn't have hurt him or anything. Your boyfriend. Neil just wanted me there as a buffer, to stop it getting out of hand.

Alex *(laughs)* As a what?

Ray Buffer. You know, minder. 'S why I left when you turned up with your sister. I thought I'm not needed here, I better get out, leave 'em to it.

Alex And leave Neil the van?

Ray thinks about that one for a while. He moves forward with a new proposition.

Ray Okay. How about this? When I get it back I'll come over and help you move his stuff out. How's that? We'll

74

dump it somewhere else. Or just get rid of it – what do you reckon? I'll take a day off, come round while he's at work, really fuck him over. I'm on your side in this. You know that, don't you?

Alex I hope so.

Ray I ain't scared of him.

Alex Okay.

Ray You wanna do it? Get rid of his stuff?

Alex No. I meant, okay, you're not scared of him.

Silence. Alex gets a saucepan to put the soup on.

Ray Where's your sister? Gone home, yeah?

Alex Not yet.

Ray Oh right. (*Beat.*) She seems nice.

Alex She's married.

Ray No, I didn't mean that. I just thought she was nice. Nice person.

Alex laughs at that. Ray comes closer, taking an interest in the kitchen design.

You've had these a while, yeah? The units.

Alex Since we moved in.

Ray Yeah, I thought so. You want to think about getting a new lot. We could do all the graphics on a computer, design it yourself –

Alex I can't afford it.

Ray No, it'd be cheap. I'd get you a discount on the materials –

Alex It's okay.

Ray And I'd do the fitting myself. You know, for free. I could come over on the weekends. Wouldn't take long.

Alex No, I couldn't –

Ray 'S no problem. I mean, I'd like to. As a sort of apology.

Alex There's no need.

Ray I wouldn't get in your way. Be five, six weekends, tops.

Alex I can't –

Ray Maybe four – you won't even know I'm here.

Alex I'm going to be moving soon.

Ray Well, that's even better, isn't it? Put a load of value on the flat –

Alex I don't want a new kitchen. (*Beat.*) Sorry. Thanks anyway.

Ray nods, gutted but trying to be nonchalant. Alex continues her preparations.

Ray Right. Well, if you change your mind, it's there, you know? I mean, I'm not doing much, I could start whenever.

Alex I'll bear it in mind. Thank you.

Ray smiles. Awkward beat. He's gearing up to declare himself – now or never. Alex knows it. The intercom buzzer sounds. Alex moves towards it as Vicky comes out of the bedroom, carrying her bag, her coat already on and buttoned up. She stares at Ray as she lights up a cigarette. Ray smiles, gesturing 'hello'.

Ray Alright?

Vicky blanks him and heads for the door. Alex is at the intercom.

Alex (*to intercom*) Hello?

Taxi Mini-cab.

Alex (*to intercom*) She'll be right down.

Ray Safe journey, yeah?

Alex turns from the intercom as Vicky starts to go.

Alex I'll phone you tonight.

Vicky Don't bother.

Alex Vicky –

Vicky I'm going to be out. So there's no point. Is there?

Alex I'll leave a message.

Vicky laughs/scoffs at her sister's overtures, looking at her scathingly. She takes another drag, exhales, blowing smoke into the flat but away from Alex.

Vicky Bye Alex.

Alex is struck by the finality of that. Vicky turns to go. Alex makes a last effort.

Alex Say hi to Mum.

Vicky goes. Alex closes the door behind her. She moves slowly back towards the kitchen, brooding, almost forgetting Ray is there.

Ray Had a row, yes?

Alex gives him a look, wanting him to go. She quickens her actions, busying herself with the preparations. Ray watches her, aware of the vibe, but enjoying being alone with her too much to act on it.

Looks healthy. You on a diet?

Alex No.

Ray No, no need, have you? I'm doing a bit. Hard though, innit?

Alex Eat less. Exercise more.

Ray I can't, can I? Crooked me knee.

Alex Swimming?

Ray Never learnt. And me Mum don't help much. Every night I get back she's got this big plate of something ready – thinks I'm ill if I don't eat it all.

Alex nods, carrying on with her work. Silence.

I should get out really. Find a new place, but it's hard, you know? Now me Dad's dead. She's really enjoying having me around. Sort of relying on me a bit.

Alex flicks a glance at him – she can relate to that. Ray interprets it as a more cynical look.

Well, and it's cheap, yeah. I can't really afford anywhere else.

Alex No?

Ray Nah. Gail put the CSA on me, didn't she? (*Scoffs.*) Fucking insult, innit? I buy everything for them kids – all the extras – on top of what I give her anyway.

Alex Yes?

Ray Yeah. New shoes, coats – there ain't a weekend when one of them's not saying, 'Mummy said you had to buy us this.' I mean, fair enough, they're my kids only now I got this bunch of arseholes telling me I got to give her even more 'cos she's struggling to make ends meet. It's just bollocks, innit? Kids are in school now, she's working again, and living with this other bloke – and he's doing alright – better than me. I mean, she ain't struggling that much if every half-term she packs the kids off to me and fucks off abroad with matey boy. I ain't had a holiday in five years – she's been to Greece, Corfu, Thailand, they even went to America once. Just them, mind, not the kids.

Alex No?

Ray No. Tell a lie. She took 'em to Spain once. They liked that. Showed me the photos and everything. Nice, that was. My wife. My kids. And him. It's not right, is it? (*Beat.*) I never hit her. Or cheated on her. I just . . . bored her. Why the fuck am I paying for that?

He realises with horror he might cry. He moves away, embarrassed. Alex has stopped her work, sympathetic now.

Fucking hell. Went off on one there. Sorry.

Alex 'S okay.

Ray What was I talking about? 'Bout me Mum, weren't it? She's fine, yeah. Is that what you asked? And the kids, yeah – yeah they're great. Kev's in the school team now. Well, in the squad, anyway. Jemma's learning the flute. Fucking pain in the arse that is, I tell you.

Alex smiles. Ray finds her gaze deeply unsettling.

D'you want any help with that? Chopping or . . .

Alex No. Thanks.

Ray Right.

Alex You can help me eat it if you like. I've made a lot.

Ray Yeah? (*Beat.*) Nah, thanks but –

Alex Splodge? It's okay. I'd like you to.

Ray Ray.

Alex What?

Ray My name's Ray. I fucking hate Splodge.

Alex Ray? Would you like to have lunch with me?

Ray I'd love to. Thanks.

Alex smiles and busies herself with the final prepar-
ations. Ray takes his coat off and hangs it up. He
comes back, desperately trying to think of something
interesting to say. He gets his fags out, then puts them
back, remembering the food. He watches Alex work.
She looks up and catches his glance, he smiles, nods,
she smiles back then carries on. He fidgets a bit,
turns his back, checks his breath with his cupped
hand. He moves back towards her.

So, who is he then? This Ben bloke? How d'you meet
him? Can I ask that?

Alex Yes, of course. I met him through Neil. They were
best friends at university.

Ray Not now though.

Alex No.

Ray What's he do?

Alex Civil engineer. He builds bridges, docks –

Ray Yeah, I know what one is.

Alex Sorry.

Ray My uncle did a bit of that.

Alex Yes? Neil started it. Dropped out, of course.

Ray Serious, is it? With Ben?

Alex Yes. I hope so anyway.

Ray Congratulations.

Alex Here.

Alex gives him a bowl of soup.

Ray Thanks. That's great.

Ray sits, waiting for her. Alex pours herself a bowl. She sits. Ray smiles at her, she smiles back. They start to eat.

I reckon we should put the cooker there. I mean, if you decide to do it. Couple of wall cabinets, give you space for a dishwasher. We'd have to chew on the colours a bit though. 'S not working like this. D'you think? It's up to you, of course, but what I think we should do is . . . probably . . .

He tails off, turning to see who Alex is looking at. Neil has entered the flat. Ray gets up, taking a step away from the table as though caught in a guilty act.

Alright?

Neil Yes, Splodge. I'm fine. You?

Ray Yeah. Yeah, I popped round for me van and Alex offered me a bit of lunch. 'S alright, innit? (*Beat.*) Where were you this morning?

Neil I've been packing all my stuff up.

Ray What about the game?

Neil What about it?

Ray Well, we needed a lift, didn't we? I mean, I was alright but I think some of the others have got a few strong opinions on the subject.

Neil (*laughs*) Did we lose?

Ray Sixteen–nil. We've been officially relegated.

Neil Excellent. (*Beat.*) Do you want to start unloading then? I want to talk to Alex.

Ray Well, it's my knee, innit?

Neil There's plenty of light stuff. Make a start on that.

Alex I'll heat it up again. Sorry, Ray. D'you mind? Please?

Ray gets up, minding very much.

Ray You got the keys?

Neil It's open.

Ray goes, not happy. He doesn't quite close the door.

Well?

Alex Well?

Neil Pregnant.

Alex That's right.

Neil Three months.

Alex It's not you.

Neil How do you know?

Alex You pulled out.

Neil I was drunk –

Alex It was four months ago and you pulled out – you did it all over my back. We couldn't even look at each other anymore.

Neil Does he know? Ben?

Alex Of course.

Neil And he's alright about it?

Alex (*beat*) He will be. Yes.

Neil What about the flat?

Alex Option one. We'll sell it, split the proceeds.

Neil And then what?

Alex I'll move in with him.

Neil Simple as that.

Alex You've got no right –

Neil (*flaring*) Don't tell me what I should fucking feel, Alex. It's not over yet.

Alex What?

Neil It's not over.

Alex Why do you do this?

Neil There's another option. One we didn't discuss.

Alex I'm not interested.

Neil Option Five. You sign the transfer form. Handing the flat over to me. All of it.

Alex stares at him, not quite able to believe what he's said.

Alex What?

Neil I'll get the form.

Neil moves to a drawer where the forms were put.

Alex We're going to sell the flat –

Neil You can't sell it unless I agree and I don't. Won't. Not ever.

Alex Option One –

Neil Is no longer available. Sorry. Options two, three and four are also off the table – there's only one left.

Alex No.

Neil You've got a nice, big house with Ben now, Alex – you've got to leave me something. It's five years of my life –

Alex Which you wasted.

Neil Not if you give me this. Here.

Neil gets out a pen and comes across with the transfer form. Alex backs off.

Alex No way.

Neil I gave you Ben, didn't I? You've got exactly what you want – now sign the fucking form.

Alex starts to walk away but Neil grabs hold of her arm. She tries to shrug him off.

Alex Get off.

Neil You're going to sign this, Alex.

Alex No.

Neil You fucking sign it!

He holds her and shakes her. Beat. She takes the form as if to comply then tears it in half.

I'll get another. You brought a lot of spares –

Neil goes to the drawer, Alex tries to get out but Neil runs across and stops her. A struggle. Ray comes in holding a small standard lamp.

Alex Get him off.

Ray What's going on?

Neil Get in. Get in.

Neil pulls Ray in and closes the door. Alex backs into the centre of the room.

Ray Look, why don't we just talk about it?

Neil That's a good idea. Here's what's going to happen. I've given Alex one of my friends to fuck and she's going to give me this flat.

Alex Ray, keep him off me while I call the police.

Neil Yeah, you do that and maybe she'll let you fuck her as well.

Alex This is stupid.

Neil Sign the form.

Alex Ray?

Ray Well, I'm confused – what's going on?

Neil She owes us, Splodge.

Alex You can't make me sign anything.

Neil No?

Alex And he's a witness that you forced me –

Neil No, he's a participant. He's going to join in, aren't you?

Ray What?

Neil lunges at Alex and grabs her. He gets behind her holding her wriggling body around the waist with one arm as he tries to grab a flailing arm.

Alex Splodge, just go. Get someone –

Neil You fucking stay here.

Alex Just go.

Neil hauls the struggling Alex over towards the door to block Ray's exit.

Ray, get him off me. Please. Ray.

Ray Come on, man. What are you doing? Don't hurt her.

Neil We're not going to hurt her. We're going to have some fun. Aren't we, babe?

Neil has succeeded in pinning Alex's arms behind her back with one hand. With the other he feels her breasts, over then under her sweatshirt. Alex struggles throughout both physically and vocally.

Oh, look at this, Splodge. Look at her. She's lovely, man. How long's it been, eh? I said, look. It's Alex.

Ray Don't . . .

Neil It's what you've always wanted. You won't ever get a chance like this. Come on.

Ray We can't . . .

Neil We're doing it. You can fuck her. Do whatever you want. Anything. We'll get away with it.

Ray Neil . . . stop it . . .

Neil I bet she's wet just thinking about it. Is that right, babe? Let's get you nice and wet, eh?

Neil licks his fingers and stuffs his free hand down her tracksuit pants. Alex's struggles and screams intensify. Ray hovers ineffectually.

Ray What are you doing? Don't. Neil. (*to Alex*) I'm sorry – I don't know what to do.

Neil She's soaking. (*Laughs.*) Splodge, I'm not lying, she's loving it, she's absolutely dripping – look.

Neil brings his hand out from her trousers and holds it out – everyone stops, horrified. His hand is wet with blood. Neil slackens his grip on Alex. She wriggles free and checks herself. Her hand comes out, similarly covered in blood. She cries out, aghast.

Ray Fucking hell. What did you do?

Neil Nothing.

Alex Oh, Christ, no. No.

Neil I didn't do anything.

Alex I've got to get to a hospital. Oh Jesus.

Ray We'll go in the van. Give us the keys.

Alex Ohhhh. God.

Ray Neil. The fucking keys, let's go. Come on. Neil?

Neil looks at them both, hesitating.

Neil Sign the form.

Ray What?

Neil Sign the transfer form first.

Alex Neil.

Ray Give us the fucking keys –

Neil You're not going 'til you've signed it. You'll lose your kid. What's more important?

Alex Give me it. Pen.

Ray You cunt.

Alex signs it.

Neil You've got blood on it. Do it again.

Alex Neil, please!

Neil (*to Ray*) Give her a fucking form.

Alex Please.

Ray gives her a form. She wipes her hands and signs it, steps away.

Ray Keys. Come on.

Neil takes the form aside and gives Ray the keys. Ray turns to Alex.

Let's go. 'S okay. You'll be alright.

Ray grabs his coat and takes the totally distraught Alex out. Beat. Neil stands there, disorientated. He looks blankly at the form, his hand, then sinks down on his haunches, choking up, feeling both sick and close to tears. Fade to black.

SCENE THREE

Evening. Everything that could have conceivably been removed to the bedroom has gone. The carpet has been pulled up exposing as much of the bare floor as possible. The lights in the flat are off but the curtains are open, enabling the moon/street light to partially illuminate the interior. Neil sits on the floor, contemplating the wreckage around him. The door buzzer sounds. And again. Neil gets up and presses the release button, opens the front door, then returns to his previous position. Beat. Ray enters, tries the light, it doesn't work. He takes in the chaos as he comes further into the flat, looks around the room, then spots Neil. Neil hasn't reacted to his presence at all.

Ray They're going to keep her in overnight. Do some more tests. Keep an eye on her.

Neil Right.

Ray She ain't lost it or anything. Not yet, anyhow. It's something to do with her cervix. They've had to stitch it up but it looks like she might be alright. 'S good, innit?

Neil Yeah.

Ray So, what I'm saying is, it was going to happen anyway. Probably. It weren't you. It was something she had wrong with her.

Neil nods in acknowledgment. Ray shifts awkwardly, a little freaked out at all this.

Her Mum and Vicky are there. Thought it best if I . . . you know? (*Beat.*) Is it alright if I use the loo? D'you mind? Sorry.

Neil shrugs and gestures: go ahead. Ray moves off to the bedroom. He stands in the doorway and tries the light. It doesn't work either. He turns to Neil.

What happened to the lights?

Neil I don't know. Broken, I think.

Ray You got a torch?

Neil What?

Ray Don't matter.

Neil I've got a lighter.

Ray Nah, it's alright. I'll manage. 'S okay.

Ray moves into the bedroom. Beat. Neil gets up, seized by an idea, and moves to the kitchen. He starts to empty the cupboards: pots, pans, foodstuffs are all dumped on a unit top as he continues his search. He stops, frustrated, then furiously sweeps all the items off the unit onto the floor.

(*off*) You alright? Neil? What's up?

The toilet flushes. Ray exits from the bedroom.

Neil There's no candles.

Ray What?

Neil I thought we had some. Under the sink. They were there.

Ray It's okay. It don't matter –

Neil I've got to see what I'm doing, haven't I? I can't clear all this up in the dark. Look at it. It's a fucking mess, isn't it? (*Beat.*) We had them. I know we did. They were there. In that cupboard.

Ray Well, maybe you –

Neil slams his hand down on the unit top with great force.

Neil Fuck it!

He takes a moment to compose himself then looks up at a very wary Ray.

Neil They were there. It was the first thing we ever bought for the flat. First evening we were here.

Ray Right.

Neil It was a Sunday night. Pitch fucking black – Alex went out to get some. No electricity, see? It hadn't been connected. We weren't even supposed to have moved in yet but, somehow, we'd got the keys so we could have a quick look round. Grab a sneak preview, you know?

Ray Yeah.

Neil (*laughs*) She was that excited about it. Couldn't wait. I mean, it was fucking basic. No phone, carpets . . . Repossession, see? We weren't happy about that, but it was all we could afford.

Ray Neil . . .

Neil What?

Ray Well, I can't stay long, I've got –

Neil Yeah, I know. I'm getting to the point, just hang on a minute, will you? So we came in, had a bit of a smooch – darker than this it was. And there were these leaflets scattered by the door, just been shoved in regardless – Indian, Chinese, pizza places – piles of the fuckers. I mean, we'd planned to go out and eat but Alex suddenly thought it'd be perfect here. More romantic. You know? First night. Candlelit supper. So we ordered a take-away on her mobile and then she went off to the shops –

Ray And that's how you know there were candles? Yeah, right, I can see that. Sure. And you kept them there, under . . . What?

Neil Am I boring you or something?

Ray No.

Neil D'you want to finish it for me? Is that it? Am I not going fast enough –

Ray I'm sorry –

Neil I'm telling a story here. Are you going to fucking listen or what?

Ray Yeah, I am. Yeah. Sorry. I didn't mean to . . .

Neil continues to stare at him as though deciding whether to attack. Ray adopts as relaxed a position as he can.

Yeah, go on. Go ahead. I'm listening.

Neil takes a beat then moves to the window to look out, brooding.

Neil?

Neil If you could have one wish – what would it be?

Ray Eh?

Neil One wish. What would you wish for?

Ray I don't know. That me kids were happy, I suppose.

Neil laughs. He turns from the window to look at Ray.

Neil No. What would *you* want? A totally, selfish, fucking wish. What do you want for you? (*Beat.*) I used to have this game with Alex. If you spotted an eyelash, loose on their cheek, side of the nose – you'd gather it up then hold it out for them to blow. Get a wish, see? We played it here that first night. She found one on me. Held it up. And I looked at her and thought . . . I wish this was enough. (*Beat.*) She used to say 'I love you' in a way that made me cringe. 'I love you, Neil' – in this whining, self-pitying tone that meant 'Don't leave me'. As though she knew, in her heart, that I wanted to go and that if she piled on enough emotional guilt maybe I wouldn't. And when I finally did I thought at least now I'll be free. At least now I won't ever hear that bleating tone again. But of course I did hear it again. Only it wasn't her saying it. It was me. 'I love you, Caroline.' 'Don't leave me.' (*Beat.*) I'd always had this arrogant sensibility that I deserved better – even leaving Alex was a kind of public declaration that I wasn't going to settle for second-rate. And here was Caroline making the same fucking declaration about me. It made me think that all those times when Alex said 'I love you,' maybe that's exactly what she meant. (*Beat.*) You'd better go.

Ray Yeah.

Ray doesn't move.

Neil What?

Ray Well, I've got your stuff, haven't I? In the van. What d'you want me to do with it?

Neil Bin it.

Ray Yeah?

Neil New beginning, eh? Fresh start.

Ray looks around at the flat.

Ray Yeah. Well, it's yours now, isn't it?

Ray starts to go. He stops at the door, deliberating whether to say it.

I think Ben might be coming round. With a few people.

Neil 'S okay. I want it.

Ray I'll see you, Neil.

Ray goes. Beat. Neil gets out a last cigarette, lights it then moves back to the window. Beat. The key sounds in the lock and Alex comes in carrying a bag of goodies: bottle of wine and a box of candles etc . . . She's out of breath with both excitement and running.

Alex It's a fantastic shop – open 'til midnight – you can get anything you want in there. Wine, food, candles . . .

Neil Al-righty.

Alex And . . .

She takes out a box of candles before delving back into the bag.

A cheap and tacky candlestick holder.

She brings it out: the description was generous. Neil laughs.

No food yet?

Neil No. They said half an hour.

Alex Can you open the wine?

Neil Sure.

Neil gets the wine out the bag as Alex starts to fix a candle into the holder.

Um, corkscrew?

Alex Oh shit.

Neil You spazz.

Alex Lucky I remembered to get one, isn't it?

She hands a corkscrew from her pocket to Neil.

Neil Here. Use this.

He hands over his lighter and starts on the wine as she lights the candle. She picks it up and looks around the room, savouring her new ownership, smiling, excited.

Alex It's great, isn't it?

Neil Yes. Small.

Alex Yes, but it's fine for now. We don't need anything bigger. Not yet. (*Beat.*) We could put a sofa bed in here, be like a spare room, then, wouldn't it?

Neil has opened the bottle and is sitting there, reflective.

What?

Neil D'you buy glasses?

Alex Of course. Not. Oh, bollocks.

They laugh. Neil takes a swig out of the bottle.

Neil Fuck it.

Alex Here. Give me it.

*She puts the candlestick holder down and takes the
bottle of wine. She has a swig and beckons him over.
She puts her mouth over his to let the wine drain from
one to another. It turns into a kiss. Alex pulls back,
both of them licking their lips.*

Mmmm. What do you think?

Neil Not bad.

Alex Again, my liege?

Neil (*beat*) It's going to be alright, isn't it?

Alex Yes. It's going to be fine.

Neil I know. Scary though.

Alex It's no different from rent. Except cheaper.

Neil Yeah. Yeah, you're right.

Alex Hey. Even if you get fired we'll be okay.

Neil Yes. Fucking bitch.

Alex Why, what's happened now?

Neil Nothing. It's just all this 'Call me Caroline' crap
while making sure you know full well who's in charge.
She was a fucking secretary at Webbers and now I'm
meant to take her shit like she's something other than an
over-promoted typist.

Alex (*laughs*) She must be good at her job –

Neil She is. And so am I. I didn't have any problems
with Russell.

Alex Well, she is quite new –

Neil If we hadn't just bought a place I'd tell her to stick
it up her arse.

Alex Don't do that –

Neil Well, I can't now, can I?

Alex I don't mean because of the flat. We'd get by. You'd find something else. It's not that, it's just, you love that job. It's the longest one you've ever stuck at –

Neil Exactly. Maybe it's time to move on –

Alex She'll settle down. She wants to make her mark, that's all.

Neil Alex. I. Fucking. Hate. Her.

Alex Two months. If it's not got any better by then, leave.

Neil thinks about that. Alex gives him a hug from behind, her head on his shoulder.

Please? For me? (*Beat.*) Here. Hold on.

She takes an eyelash from his cheek and holds it up.

Make a wish.

He looks at her, makes his wish, blows. Beat. She smiles and hugs him even tighter.

I love you, Neil.

Neil takes forever to respond.

Neil I love you too.

Fade to black on lights. The candle gets blown out.

Printed in Great Britain
by Amazon